Also Dark

Also by Angelique Palmer

The Chambermaid's Style Guide

Also Dark is a work of unapologetic transparency and intimate vulnerability. Angelique Palmer unabashedly transmutes shame, guilt, and all the little imperfections of her world (and the ones life has thrown her) into a raucous work of art. This book does not ask to take up space—it just does— brilliantly balanced in all its shadows and all of its light.

— Pages Matam, *The Heart of a Comet*

Do not be fooled by the title of Angelique Palmer's newest collection of poems. Though the dark is emphasized, in the tradition of Rumi, Palmer is well aware that "the wound is where the light enters you." Palmer's poems speak of the deep bruises of longtime wounds; some physical and marrow deep, and others that are etched into the soul. However, Palmer deftly wields her wry humor and utilizes Clifton like discernment, to craft a body of poems that offer unflinching vulnerability, tangible, lush desire and an irrepressible hunger to shoulder the healing after the harm. These poems leak light and make you, dear reader, that much braver to meet tomorrow after reading them.

— Derrick Weston Brown, *Wisdom Teeth and On All Fronts; Floodgate Poetry Series Vol. 5*

Also Dark strikes between the extremes of affirmation and survival. These poems linger and speak like a sister-friend climbing out of the rough to find cotton candy, the perfect sweater dress, and skies that let women stretch into the future.

— Tara Betts, *Break the Habit*

This title by Angelique Palmer is a vulnerable collection that almost feels like a coming-of-age journey. It is brilliant work that is full of tragic emotional experiences and hopeful self-realization. Readers will find themselves unraveling and then tangled in her ability to perfectly paint pain, resilience, forgiveness, and joy.

— Douglas Powell/Roscoe Burnems, First Poet Laureate of Richmond, VA

Also Dark

Angelique Palmer

Etruscan Press

Etruscan Press
Wilkes University
84 West South Street
Wilkes-Barre, PA 18766
(570) 408-4546

www.etruscanpress.org

Published 2021 by Etruscan Press
Printed in the United States of America
Cover art: Terri A. Meredith, Visual Artist. Series title: *Milage*. Digital rendering title: *Mokara*
Cover design by Carey Schwartzburt
Interior design and typesetting by Todd Espenshade
The text of this book is set in Baskerville.

First Edition

17 18 19 20 5 4 3 2 1

Library of Congress Cataloguing-in-Publication Data

Names: Palmer, Angelique, 1972- author.
Title: Also dark / Angelique Palmer.
Description: Wilkes Barre, PA : Etruscan Press, 2021. | Summary: "Searching
    for a singular voice in one's own mind must be incredibly boring, or exhausting.
    But, by paying attention, author Angelique Palmer finds music in the many
    committee presiding over her thought life: there's a fantastic loop of wonderful
    jazz piano listing in the hum of one, an intelligent gibberish in the brilliant scat
    of another, the screaming brass of a blaring trumpet in a third, a simultaneous
    strand plays foot candle to cradle the shadows it casts and still another culls a
    timbre of comedy only survivors understand to be Also Dark. And that's only
    scratching the surface"-- Provided by publisher.
Identifiers: LCCN 2021004652 | ISBN 9780989753272 (paperback)
Subjects: LCGFT: Poetry.
Classification: LCC PS3616.A3388245 A79 2021 | DDC 811/.6--dc23
LC record available at https://lccn.loc.gov/2021004652

Please turn to the back of this book for a list of the sustaining
funders of Etruscan Press.

Foreword

So your lungs,
 full of ocean,
that's the way you were born
and your mouth,
full of water,
 that's the way you speak life,
this is your boat,
we are your water,
So every time you get sucked in,
You just gotta relearn how to swim.

I first encountered Angelique in Abiquiu, New Mexico, during the August 2015 AROHO ("A Room of Her Own") annual writing retreat and workshop series. A month before the retreat, I'd been diagnosed with a brain aneurysm, which required surgery. Even as I knew I would fear each bump of turbulence on the plane, each hard stop on the bus leading to the Ghost Ranch, concerned that those jolts would induce rupture, I elected to travel to Georgia O'Keefe's haven because I believed something there awaited me.

For two weeks, I participated in workshops, readings, and I met a number of remarkably talented women writers, women warriors tearing through the page; however, the majesty of the AROHO retreat, the beauty of O'Keefe's sacred space had all but escaped me. Maybe because my every thought was on the months that lay ahead, the doctor's visits, the years my children would spend without me if I were lost on the surgery table, the ways my body, my mind would be erased if the doctor just sneezed, if some miscalculation of meds erased the very essence of me. I stood in one of the most beautiful places on earth, in the company of some of the most remarkable women, untouched, disconnected until I experienced Angelique Palmer.

This quiet, unassuming, small amongst so many big egos, big mouths, big words, she moved along the ranch almost transparent. In fact, I hadn't seen her, beyond my grief, before I saw her on the stage: locked hair down her back, lady in red sundress, big, but not big enough to obscure her weightiness, weightlessness, gold sandals as her words vaulted out of her, and her red dress became a cape, she rose above, but with us, became one with us all, sweeping over the room, a wave. We didn't stand a chance. We had all been transformed. It is she, Angelique, goddess who rocked the room, rocked me out of my fear, commanded I swim, commanded I relearn, that I remember that with which I had been born, that I could still, no I *must* continue to speak life, into others, into myself.

Fast forward to 2020, five years removed from the Ghost Ranch, the essence of our country, at risk of being erased, of being something different. Etruscan Press offers me the gift of voice of word, to procure a manuscript of an African American writer who could sing in such turbulent times. Immediately, without hesitation, Angelique … Angelique, her water, her ocean, she could speak to us all. Her words could remind us, bid us to remember to relearn, to swim.

— Laurie Jean Carter, author of *Crave: Sojourn of a Hungry Soul*
(Etruscan Press, 2015)

January 20, 2021

Writing about what you know is boring.
Writing what you don't know about what you know.
That requires investigation.

~ Lauren Rusk

For Magali:
Thank you for saving my life.

For My Family, blood & chosen:
You make life worth living every day.

Acknowledgments

Laurie Carter

Douglas C. Powell

Camisha Jones

Pages Matam and the Beltway Poetry Slam

Dr. Simone Roberts

Wheeler Light

Monifa Lemons, Candace Wiley and the Watering Hole Writing Retreat

and Open Mic Nights everywhere

TABLE OF CONTENTS

Passive Voice on a Tuesday

Won't you come celebrate with me
What I have shaped into
A kind of life?
I had no model.
Born in Babylon
Both nonwhite and woman
                          - Lucille Clifton

Witness all I have survived
How each thing has teeth lungs eyes
How all of them assassins
of poor aim
How all of them left the way they came

Really, come see...
My molesters- as monsters
My bullies, their bruises
My childhood made of pitfall, tried   failed

No, you want it? Then come see...
My poverty like suffocation
daddy issues like gut punch
anorexia like'ta swallow the whole of me   failed

Come see...
my alcoholism
Low self-esteem
my rapist, and his ghost   failed

The cis-men who would ignore the glory that is
this black
and strong
and woman;
who only understand me as target for their lust or their hate.

If I'm truthful,
my mind has come the closest,
So I don't need you to kill me
I was born with every thought that can end me
Which means I contain everything I need to survive this- to survive you

You?!
How you brought your petty to my pen game   and failed!
Stand me in front of a mirror
                    I'll strike a pose
Sit me in front of my demons,
                    I'll lick his nose
Show me a clock or a calendar
                    I'll show you my growth
Once provoked,
I'll find a way to eviscerate
            the real work of me ain't done.

You think you can tell my story better than I can?   No.
Stand in front of me and spit some shit you ain't lived? No.
You think you can character assassinate me into silence?
            No.   NO!

Until you do right by me
you'll have an infinite amount of Mama Lucille's chiming light
    grinding into your soul…

Come celebrate with me
that everything
        everything
                EVERYTHING
has tried to kill me…   and it's just
another Tuesday!

All of the Above

"When we speak, we are afraid our words will not be heard or welcomed.
But when we are silent, we are still afraid. So it is better to speak." - Audre Lorde

Maybe I only talk when I have something important to say.

Maybe I don't talk because
    I'm my Mother's 3rd daughter
        Talked Over,
        Talked At,
        and Talked Down To
    I'm my Mother's 3rd daughter
        Can't be out there looking stupid
        Shouldn't be out there spreading my business
        DON'T ever be Loud and Wrong
            Don't be wrong
                research,
                then research your research
                research that shit again
            Don't be loud
                Who you think you talking to?
                      challenging your elders can get you smacked
                Being woman black and loud can get you killed, because
                      She was being uppity
                      She was being saddity
                      She was taking up room (see also: why to be small and quiet)

I'm my Mother's 3rd daughter
cursed with her loneliness
Maybe I don't talk because
I don't think I have anything important to say because
I've always made everyone more important than I was,
smarter than I am,
more powerful than I could ever be
(even if this is untrue it's me being honest:)
Here's my opinion at a discount because
I don't want you to argue with me,
I don't argue well,
I trauma into silent.
Black women, with trauma? (see also: pray it away)
Maybe I don't talk because
it makes me unattractive to a dwindling pool of suitors that are no longer checking for me
my emotions are a situation
my body's crumbling
my good looks waving in the rear-view mirror
perhaps my looks will be attacked (more brutally than I attack them)
perhaps my nerve will be attacked (like she's got some nerve lookin' like she do…)
I'm my Mother's 3rd daughter
her curse is my loneliness
Maybe I don't talk because
when I do people say the exact same thing as I and get more credit.
Black women are stolen from all the time
Black women's opinions are discounted all the time
Black, woman, and old is a clearance aisle item now
I'm my Mother's 3rd daughter
my curse is my loneliness
my isolation convinces me I'm a clearance item, pennies a pound
I trauma into silent

Maybe I only talk when I have something important to say

Maybe all
of the above.

Wither

I have been trying to tell you of my rotten teeth,
or how I used to drink, but not anymore.
How that doesn't mean damage undone

I have been trying to tell you of my rotten teeth.
How recovering girls look like oyster shells, no meat or pit
an iridescence in their ascent, but jagged still.

I have been trying to tell you of my rotten teeth
before we kiss
I want you to know
I see the wither in my left front tooth
I know the candy hearts behind the zombie enamel
the gutting and cracked ones,
the crooked and worn ones.
I know how a dying nerve and un-swallowed blood
turns my exhale into July on the leaf of a Corpse flower
I don't want you to kiss me without knowing I know
or knowing I don't think I deserve
to be kissed.
When I was drunk,
and hurting I neglected myself expertly.
Now it shows in my smile, in
my silence, in how I keep my affection to myself.
If you choose to kiss me
I might linger a little long.
Recovered lovers don't get kissed too often
I swallow my blood, cover my smile,
punish my wither with an unfair amount of want.

I'm rotting away, pretty sure this is what I deserve.
If you choose not to kiss me
I'm pretty sure, I deserve this too.

If Someone Decided I Was Trash

10 years ago, I would have agreed with them
Taking up their precious clean rose-smelling atmosphere
to explain why I am so sorry for being the refuse they refuse to understand
bent at the waist over and over
asking them to validate and forgive me
It is after all, all about me.

If someone decided I was trash
5 years ago, I would have walked away from them.
Unsure why my *Recovery Spell* had worked on everyone but them.
Why my cloak failed to fool; what is their special, their inoculation?
Attracted to and repelled by them.
It is about them now.

If someone decided I was trash
2 years ago, I would contemplate the life choices that lead to their inner corruption.
In a separate thread I would collect my faults to shine them glossy
with all of the ways broken people have caused me emotional damage,
with all of the ways I returned their sharp
Third simultaneous thought: People are not disposable.

Sometimes people are unhealthy or toxic   and need to leave.
Sometimes they need to grow.
You need to leave to let them do so.
Sometimes people are just being people.
And thems is not your people.
It's about finding your people.
If someone called me trash today
I'd be like…

…you're better than that trash metaphor though.

For the House at 1133 Flanders Street New Orleans, LA 70114

I hear you be the block, but I'm the lights that keep the streets on
~Beyonce Knowles

When I am street,
I'm the street where I lived

I am lamp light pattern all the way home
on repeat where I live

I'm the cement sidewalk cracks
'round the weeds where I live

I'm the trunk of useless inheritance
replete with where I live

I'm the run-off puddles collecting what
we secrete where I live

How we loved, spit and shit and talk it
so deep where I live

I'm the all spent and spending- ends
need to meet where I live

I'm an 8-peg Legos building
reds and greens where I live

I am Nanny's DNA shine
unsheathed where I live

Black body, black blight and
black gris gris where I live

Been the block since I was born.
Soul I seek is where I live.

When I am the most myself,
I'm the street where I live.

Wanna See?

I'm from passion and known
    from bad and woman
    from message and physical
I'm a delicious ballet

I'm from greed and follow
      from stop and watch
      from fast and way   and run away, fast.

I'm from passion and know
      from they and I
      from magic and sweat
      from want and this
      from know enough to know

On any given day I'm
a hive of stinging
a drown of tears
a throat of bones
a belly of electricity
a swallow of profanity

Might be
a scream made of throb
a storm made of smile
a sex made of heaven

Yes, I am
a heaven of hand-holds
a warmth of loss
a cooling of the loss leaving
a vibration of cares to give
a petal of caresses

a caress of incantations
a progenitor of cures
a cure of eclipses
an eclipse of tears
a stinging of hives

At the corner of rise and fall
I'm from precise mist and too wild a burn
I'm a revenge of voices
Wanna see?

Come with me.

Neva Scared

But for real,
I really wish a muthafucka would part their lips to tell me HOW to be a
black woman in this world
I would say
What took you so long,
been here a minute
had to figure the shit out myself.   You're
welcome.
I would say
you seriously have the unmitigated gall to address me as anything
lower than heaven
and expect me
not to end you?
I would say
Who is you?
Who your people?
And most importantly,   did anybody from this side send
for you?
Huh?

HUH?!

I would say
Too many times, I let it go, let it slide, or let it fly
because I needed to hold on,
needed to slip through,
or because your thoughts were for the birds anyway.
Now I am old enough,
wise enough,
or just don't give a fuck enough,
So go, slide, and fly ain't Who you get to today
You get Me.

And I'm saying:
> There's nothing about you, that cannot be corrected,
> by you.
>> Now say sorry.
>> And leave.

I come from a long line of Aunties, we ain't neva scared.

God or a Lottery Ticket in a Black Woman's Purse

  Trying to find faith
in a world that is slowly killing me and blaming me for why they can't do
it right

or why survival might be the only thing in the way of enjoying life

or the privileges I own are many but the luxury of using them correctly
belong to someone else

or suffer the little children...   that's it.

or explaining to your body that
cigarettes and alcohol use may have primed it for toxicity,
   but it's the paycheck to paycheck,
   hand to mouth, constant inconsistency
that's really stretched your survival practices into a sustenance of stressed out

or dodging the landlord, ducking my debtors, and flirting with the bill
collectors created in me
a matching set of fissures & fault lines that saying *boo*, might irreparably break

or how do you pray when you keep failing every religion that has failed you

or winning the lottery would really solve a lot of these problems,
so buying my lottery ticket is a sort of worship:
look at how every few days I ask something invisible to do something
impossible,
how that is a living joy

or faith is the only thing keeping me alive,
when the world isn't...

Supernova

My whole life my mother has been the strongest woman I know. **A**
Supernatural Mother-something able to bend time with her will. **Black**
and loud enough to warp walls with her anger, leave a **hole**
where the plaster was weak. Wields power with just a look, she **is**
getting older though. She keeps everything for a reason type of older: **a**
book of pictures, a paper weight, random jar of dirt from some **place**.
Reasons I don't get to know. She's never met a stray she wouldn't bring **in**
and has never brought in something she had **space**
for. Hoards with love. And when she began to forget **where**
she was, losing time we, lost our **gravity**.

Now Mama finds rage every day; she pushes and **pulls**
us in. And we her stars are left powerless, **so**
often. We're floating into the rush of so **much**
darkness, into unchartered horizons, into a chaos **that**
neither I, nor my sisters could **even**
prepare for. My Mama is our **light**
collapsing. What will this do to our gravity? **Can't**
tell how her aperture closing will affect the photo we **get**
A better depth of field means better exposure when the pictures come **out**.

Now, I sift so many of her pictures, people I don't know, to see if **this**
is what keeps her here; hope this sparks a light, see if something **happens**
"You never know with these things," doctors say, "You never know **sometimes**
it   just   might   happen **when**
no one's looking or counting on it." But my Mama is **a**
whole world doc, she is not just some shooting **star**.
The picture develops clearly, and the truth in the portrait **is**
No matter how strong we shine, we are all slowly **dying**.

The To-Do List in Which I Get Socks and Gather Resilience

-Pay the car note
-Make tuna tartare
-Find the value in staying put
-Take my vitamins
-Drink water
-Buy true matching foundation make-up
-Cross-examine my shame
-Core the pineapple
-Decide what I'm going to be when I crone up
-Try that spinach and pineapple smoothie recipe
-Seize my power
-Put my foot on the neck of my suicidal ideation
-Call on the North Wind
-Boil the ginger
-Curse my ex with an exhale of a thousand hungry sharks
-Meditate
-Put my foot on the neck of my suicidal ideation, again
-And again
-Kick the fucker to sleep
-Decide I'm not going to die alone
-Call my Mom
-Change the calendar
-Shop for renter's insurance
-Research rose water and where one keeps a thousand sharks
-Get a new therapist
-Buy socks, comfortable ones

A Psalm for the Gray Hair in My Mirror

When I start to erase myself
into an afterthought,
there *you* go…
I will call you anything you want,
if you like
I can call you "gray."
Or, and this is just a suggestion,
I can call you
> *MIRROR BALL!*

I can call you ghost of the widow's peak
I can call you glitter fleck
> pebble or stone
> fog or flint
> a solid smoke
> or the exhaled genius.

I can call you Sleep When You're Dead Gray,
I can call you the Beauty Industrial Complex Has Enough Victims Gray,
I can call you Girl Getting Good at Being a Woman Gray.
or I can call you overcast sky gray and this-
this is my favorite!
Because that way you will be   as big as the sky.
And I'll have to learn to be   as big as the sky.

And I will be the sky
to someone
even if
it's just
> …myself

So, I Says to Safi

So I says to Safi, "Safi, you know that lady? She read my cards out there."

And I don't remember exactly what she said to me, but it was probably something like, "Oh word?"
And we did that dance around it at first, that dance that says: "you don't have to tell me what she said unless you're comfortable telling me because I don't want to know unless you want me to know and I kinda do wanna know but not unless you wanna tell me…"

Then I said, "She told me I wasn't going to find true love as long as I'm sick and not taking care of it."

You ever see a thrown rock hang in the air right before it smashes something into the shards of what used to be?

Safi… did not say that. She said, "DAMN!" I agreed, expounded, "The deeper discussion though was about my motives for wanting someone in my life. Maybe I know that I need to go ahead and have the hysterectomy, and I'm afraid to go through that alone, that I will be undesirable to anyone after the fact." Here, I'm telling my friend I arrived…   broken, I can be the shards. But also the rock and the hand that throws it.
"But that Lady said, 'it isn't entirely fair to ask someone, especially someone new to hold all of that for me.'
"All the rocks   and the throwing   and the fear of what's yet to be out of fear that I cannot hold it all   myself.
"Even if I try not to, Safi, it may still end up happening since my motives are motivated by fear."
Safi said, some other really profound shit. I said, "The Lady gave me good advice, right? So, I'm moving on it. Except… knowing I have wayward motives

does not	put down
the fact	that I am
physically	and emotionally
lonely.	

This is not where I thought I would be in my life.

It is all so unfair.

I think right then I dropped the rock. Or became the glitter of glass abandoning any chance at mend. Or both.

Safi said, "It's good that you have plan, you're taking care of yourself, and know what to do next. And you must know you're never going to be alone. We're never going to let that happen Angelique."

And I kinda nodded that I know.

Except	I don't
except	I'm scared.
except	I know.
I know.	

Post Op

The pain in my belly is not an imaginary thing.
The wound is sealed skin, raised bumpy and new slice hot.

The sutures inside, a spacewalk below my navel, above the bone.
My body, an actual taken apart that's been put back together.

And when I weep, it isn't for very long.
I know this science as miracle.

I am knitting myself a patch over the bruise.

I will not miss the pain
that has not late-night lover called me.

I do hear too often on the wind... *useless*.
Like less of a woman is a light I've swallowed into the whole of me...

The only distraction is the way I hold my hand to my belly
to imagine my healing and dream of spacewalks

Pretty Picture

Picture a tortoise that's turned itself over:
legs in the air, arms-   a confused choreography of functional flail
neck trying to leverage itself to right the shell.
Anything but aggravate the new scar. Anything at all.
That was me, for like two minutes-   two minutes ago.

It was hilarious.

Several Reasons (in no particular order) Why One Should Not Order False Teeth from the Internet

1.   They have never seen your teeth
They don't know the degree of your decay   how you've held it off with a violent persistence and chastised your habits into a pitiless inner monologue

2.   They have never seen your teeth
They don't know that you know how to bear them; you are not some simple row of plastic hokum; that your jaw stretch is not a threat but probably the last thing your prey will know of life. Ain't that the strength *they* can't sell back to *you?*

3.   They have never seen your teeth
 They don't know the grace in your smile; how you will call light to kiss wind with a head tilt and giggle. How you forget your smile is broken because it repairs so many hearts. And they don't know that some people call that godstuff. You are godstuff, unique. You were never one-size fits all. You could never fit into a too-tight grift, imperfect perfidy, when everyone knows your name by the way you sing it.

4.   They have never seen your teeth
They don't know you will bite down when necessary, to withstand pain, only a lifetime of survival can teach you. They don't know you lived, worked, and became while in 20-years of pain, like the throb in your gums is a beat you've come to take your own pulse to. Or that you pulled your own tooth once. And this is after you quit drinking. You know, just you a pair of pliers and a pep talk. But woman aren't you tired of your tough enough yet? Don't you see a pattern? One that a lazy promise of instant fix simply won't address.

5.   They have never seen your teeth.

Ways in Which the Bigger Than Me Teaches Me, A Tiny Human Thing, the Concept of Specificity

I.
And the prayer probably sounded like child making Christmas list simple:
The prayer was probably thankfulness,
genuine or otherwise followed by
a stark lamp on the everything
I want and haven't got
The prayer was probably capped off
with guilt for even asking, but
a reiteration for want,
then a bargaining, for if I get it.
The prayer will probably sound trite to some,
but it was exactly, kinda like this:
I'm adored by my bloodones.
I am cherished by my chosen.
And I have gratitude for all of it—
the ones who came and left, the people who stay and stayed staying.
But, to be loved.
to be for real loved…

then I probably rubbed a lamp or said Amen.
And then the day happens, where I go about seeking but not looking for
-one is a better story than the other-
And then, while in the Wal-Mart self-checkout
buying supplies for the afternoon's classroom art project, a pair
of copulating bugs
crashed into my face. MY FACE!
Which naturally lead to
a silent screamfest, swat-fu session,
that had to make anyone who saw it
weep with laughter
ending with the two "busy bugs" landing in my open purse.

I scooped them out, paid, and left,
hoping there isn't video tape evidence of this.
(There definitely is video tape evidence of this.)

II.
I woke up this morning mooning a prayer.
And the prayer probably sounded like
Why am I not good enough for love?
Why does everyone I know get second and third and fourth chances at
admiration, affection,
at attention- romantic- from all the other human beings
Why am I invisible to sexual attention?
Inept at flirt? Too much of or not enough?

Why am I so unlovable?

The prayer probably sounded like
Why can't I fall in love?
But then,
LOVE FELL ON ME.
I think this is how the Universe teaches grace,
and specificity.

So now the prayer sounds like:
Send me your best, ready and willing
and I will love them like I loved those bugs —
enough to set them free in spite of their diligence and spared awareness for their
surroundings;
Send me your best, and I will love them like
-like I loved the lesson-
into a gentle testament to survival.
Send me your best, and I will love them like
like I loved myself
into my favorite story to tell.

A Table Read

Fade In:

Narrator:

This is an actual conversation between our hero and all the parts of her brain

Splash cut to:

Interior Car:

We find our hero cutting a swath from Louisiana to Virginia (and the several red states between) the night after the 2016 election. After several hours of silence, real and internal our hero speaks :

My Brain:

WOW! I am horny af.

Also my Brain:

No you're not.

MB:

Um I'm not? Check again.

AMB:

You're not.

MB:

HOW?!

AMB:

You really want someone to kiss you, touch you- to show you that you are real, your pain is valid. You want your black, queer, woman body to feel good in all the states you have to drive through. You want someone to make you okay.

MB:

Oh.

OH.

AMB:

Other than that, you're the regular amount of horny.

MB:

I checked with the rest of the brain. None of us like you.
NONE OF US!

Flirting

Turn your whole body to her smile
give in to your colors, if you find them there.
You'll find them there. You are every color when she shines.
And when you drop your eyes, do so gently
a bow on strings: soft, not shrill.
They say it is simple.
But she is beautiful, and you are clumsy
with simplicity, with words
you haven't rehearsed the awkward out of

Hand against her corona when you realize
She is shine, and you—
You are mood.

But, ask her.
Ask.
Please   be brave.

On Listening to Meshell Ndegeocello in the Workplace

Make sure you are alone
That there is no rainstorm
That there are no slow songs— only up tempo
That there is no pulse in her bass notes
        that mimics the pulse in your bass notes
That you don't pronounce it: horny
That you say nothing so gauche
That you are quiet with your secrets
Make sure
you are
alone
That you don't know her moan
That you don't identify with her moan
That you don't wish you made her moan
That you don't moan
That you swallow your sexuality

Make sure you don't begin to wish

That the corners of your eyes can catch
your abandoned wishes
That the shift in your panties can cover
the fickle of emotion
That you don't touch your skin in that way
that gives you away

Make sure you are not actively thinking!
That you don't look for hidden meaning,
where there is none
or think about the one you cannot touch

That you don't regret in pattern

That you can hope
when you hope
someday
you'll hope
you are
not
Alone.

Hands, Hair

I think I like the idea:
your hands,
my hair

I've been looking at your hands
and
touching my hair
all night

I've been
imagining
the place
your fingers
will find home
      be fluent in
      caress
will curse my stubborn
      stay
      unraveling this
      enigma
will sing the praise
      of kinks and curls
      of pooled oil
      and ill-positioned knot
will be snagged
      give gentle yank,
      get curdled snarl.

When we both
know the rules,
                    we can break them.

My scalp
and skin
craves
the chorus of quakes
your
way over there
hands
could deliver.

I've been
looking
at your
hands
and
touching my
hair
all night…
pretending
I'm magnet,
you,
already
here.

The Way Fire Works

Flash and grip, you pour yourself into
the smoldering dark- dizzied
from the juice of that soft-warm
    tryna control my high off tongue, flitting
from the kinetic and concentric- rings going out
like sound. And I can see them
reaching for our oxygen supply.

Wait... can I do that with you? Shimmer
a caress across your cheek,
like you do me? Could I ever match
you taste for thought?
We're gonna just stand here in the Muses at dawn,
in the thin, gauzy blankets of what we can do to each other,
torn between the physical and the morning coming in?
Oh woman please!
Can I do this with our now?
You gonna let me?

This the way fire works
Flash and grip, you pour yourself into an us-made rhythm,
a joy-joy undulation, control the burn. Glow.
You scream your certainty into my mouth the way, I melt in yours.
I bet that's all the oxygen I will ever need.

A Recipe or Conjure

1/2 cup Lust, part salted by time completely melted by the
glances across the room
1 tablespoon of brushing against each other like magnets drawn
and repelled
1 1/8 cup of the sweetest kisses (deep or passionate like lips
embracing)*
2 large cups of vulnerability
2 teaspoons pure patience extract
1/2 cup all-purpose communication
1/2 cup unsweetened balance
1/4 teaspoon intentionality
Honey to taste
Set your expectations before you start to mix

Mix the lust into a light fluffy flirt; set aside.
The main dish should be taken slow: fold what we both have into what
we both want.
We'll be made from learning each other. We'll be learning each other
while we make. One ingredient informing the other; one may chide more
than it blends remember they stay in conversation with each other. Take
a taste: is it sweet? Spicy? A challenge to what is usually a tame palette.
Add more kisses if it's working.
Check your flirt. Keep it light. And when we've stayed in the moment
long enough never rushing or comparing the mix to any one else's; when
we feel like we can fully be ourselves around each other, we'll be ready.
Are you ready?
Add back the flirt, and a generous amount of honey to taste.
Serve warm. Always pay attention to the temperature.

Tallahassee, 1998

Making a Mother Sauce in your kitchen:
It is Saturday afternoon,
tomatoes and heat, we are chopping them up.
We are sweetening the boil with
    cut basil, dry
parsley, white sugar.
 I rinse off a wooden
spoon. We get giddy about
something you said. I
scrape the sides and bottom. We wash
the butcher board more tickled than most.
I add the sweated
sweet onion. You are near the sink.
I add a big pinch of the spicy mix.
You are near my neck.
I add more tomatoes.
You lean against me, chest to my back
chin on my shoulder
zipper on my ass, tighter.

The kitchen is the smallest it has been all day.

Little pops of red-orange
 play pointillism on the
counter and against the back
splash. And I want to…

throw my color and salt to
jazz against your tongue.
But will
Everything
burn just so you
can get a taste?

After A Good Long Walk

You were inspired by the
flowers, I think.
We were holding hands.
Everything there, all clear green
pink young, noisy for silent.
You turned to me,
wiped the sides of your mouth
-I liked the sides of your mouth so I noticed
every time-
once with your thumb and forefinger
twice with the back of your other hand.
I could tell you were working your
courage into one place:
down from your brain, up
through your chest into your
mouth. You asked,
Can we be lovers?
No one has ever... asked.

I am the pervert who saw the sexy in this
new-alive garden
thought the flowers were terribly forward, showing off all of their
ecology; the peeking buds on the fresh tree
limbs like nipples through a thin shirt.
I imagined the back of your hand
on the side of my face
I imagined your thumb and forefingers
separating me.

The roll in my hips demanding I get
as good as I give.
It made the soft grass bed look
invitational, and this breeze,
made gentle was
            just for feeling,
I felt something in this
sumptuous lude of our long
springtime walk, as erudite
as sun hitting us full on
in the naughty
expecting us to sprout
and pollinate   too.

Then, I realized I haven't spoken in a minute.
You asked a question and I went inside of me.
Your face turned discouraged drooped further in my hands
And I can do nothing
but smile,
Lovers?
My Darling, we already are.

Codeword

    I woke in the armpit of you.
Your bicep, my carnival midway prize
your knee is waving from
a parade float perch and
a deviant toe finds
warm in the fleshy of my opposite calf muscle.
We are still trying
to find a way
to occupy the same space and be our own person.

You bring up caramels.
I mention my friends who divorced.
You're telling me how the caramels in the dish are *so* cool:
the dish, still a dish, upon opening the lid
is also a vessel for delicious sugary cream creations.

The dish
is even better- you explain-
because they make the caramels look
bigger, *more appealing* from the outside
than they might actually be.
What I hear is
I make you look good.
                     You're welcome.
The dish and the gold wrapped candies-   you say,
shelve well
and wake up that way.

With half a jaw of toothpaste
you ask me to elaborate
on divorce and the jigsaw puzzle we woke up as,

I tell you about my friend
who found *the love of her life!*
How she butter-stirred sweetness
around that boy, let
her tongue wrap him in golden foil
twisted it a thousand times closed
until we were fooled by the
thick glass candy dish...

until she vanished into it. She must have woken up
a thousand nights inside of him
never knowing what was inside of him
       could kill her spirit,
       leave cavities.
       make her disappear…

No one knew she was being hurt.
I didn't know. And I have a temper and
a taste for revenge.
You say negativity;
I say I'm a realist, plain speaking.
You say, *plain is bland.*
I say cavities are painful!
You say change the recipe:
       More butter, less cinnamon
       Less games more prizes
       More faith
I say faith?
You nod yes…
I say: I believe in you.

I would rather wake
a splay of limbs
in inordinate direction
than disappear
into anything I'm
supposed
to be.
I do not think I am worthy of gold foil.
But I don't think I'm vanishing either.
I like waking up in your arms.

You smile and say, *coffee?*
A codeword for
you wouldn't have us any other way.
I say, *caramel?*
A codeword for
I am actually falling for you
We say *both.*
Like we say *WE...*
Like I hope it is   you   there when I land.

On the Mysteries of Cotton Candy

Dear Person I Would Like to Remain Friends With:
I was wrong.
There's a cotton candy machine in the back of my throat. It is all sugar
and cloud. I like sugar. Not everyone does.

A man touched my hips two weeks ago, rather incidentally, and reminded
me I had hips. And skin. And that I like to be touched. When I met him
in the daylight, his smile went flat. I am so tired of being after midnight
hips. I didn't feel like that with you. Maybe because it is always sunshine,
never daylight.
Maybe I got confused.

Your default avatar in my phone is a picture of you smiling so hard, you
warm my face. I been smiling, because you been smiling, a lot.

I thought you were playing. I thought *we* were playing. I thought I felt you
yank my ponytail. It is my tradition to then give chase, but never catch.
Always get caught, don't act like that's what I wanted all along. It is a
hard habit to break.

I have slick wrists and good technique. I can spin pink grains of hope
into a puffy fantasy so expertly, in nothing flat. I think, "Look at what I've
done! Even I want a bite!" I expected you to bite. Not everyone does.

I have mood swings. I don't slide into My Dark as much anymore as I:
> use feet for brakes,
> pull myself to stand,
> walk back up the   slide.

But My Dark figured out my fake-out. Now, I flip quicker than a trick
wrist. I am sure the moods could be controlled by the medication I don't
want prescribed to me. Little pink pills that won't let me feel.

When I valley, I don't want anyone near that brand of stuck.
What if I got some of it on them?
**You ever seen what happens to cotton candy when it gets
caught in the rain?** I have been telling every single one of my friends,
so I wouldn't say it to you first. Better to mask face than have to save it.

You are a good person.
You write full-speed baseball bats to my chest.
Your heart a beautiful landscape: all peaks
and valleys, weather and carnival too.

You have a smile that draws the giggle out of this self-centered, kind,
gentle and usually hot-mess of a woman; you crush my capital I's into
lowercase grains of sugar and make me spin.

I said I would stop, and I am still thinking about you.
Turns out, I'm not a very good "friend" at all. I'm trying to be.

Sincerely,
After Midnight Hips.

Duck

I broke my ankle in 2017,
At a dodge ball game
In the school gym where I was
As the phys-ed teacher's substitute.

I caught one dodge ball to the jaw
while another slithered under
my right foot. Top of me went one way,
the bottom of me went another,
and it must have been high comedy.
Hell, I would've laughed if I saw it.
Until I went to stand up…

I couldn't put any pressure on it.
I scooted on my tush back to where
one might say I should have been
the whole time. And when I took off
the shoe, it blew up twice its size.
From there… it's a long story

Mike Tyson once said everyone has a plan until they get punched in the face.

You ever try to stand up after life catches you in the jaw but good?
See your ego in a puddle of collect-your-stuff and get-where-you-sup-
posed-to-be, girl.
The snake whispering that the apple is soft but that velocity though
And don't you know everything you need to know now,
Enough to tell when it's gonna rain way before any report
Enough to feel pressure even if it's just implied
Enough to never trust where you plant your feet
Enough to laugh at anyone who thinks life fights fair

Enough to never know if
        it's the threat of, the memory of, or the actual pain, blinding you
a ready kind of awake
Enough to always have a plan

I broke my ankle in 2017. So maybe
this is not about the one who used to beat the shit out of me.
One changed the way I walk through the world.
The other's a long story.
But if you ever see a dodgeball   or a fist   coming at you

duck.

First One to Flinch

First one to flinch
gets to wear the other's pain around their neck.
A wish-meat sandwich latch key or
the survivor's shibboleth:
I dare you
I double dare you
I double dog dare you
          PHYSICAL CHALLENGE.
Okay, then
fix the oxygen about you
in a way that it forgives
your vulnerability in it
while it respects your authority over it. No?
Then gather your squirrely nerves into a bundle.
Pocket them into a skin deeper than
what they think they can get to
what they think they can purchase
than what of you they think they already own.
No? Then be 10.
In order to play
flinch
lock eyes
with the blinding light in front of you
and floor it.
Remember
you're only as weak as the softest of your flesh
only as weak as how much you are fetching
only as weak as the backhand you knew
or should have know
was coming
coming at you
here it is
don't move.

The first one to flinch
better know how to get a running start for the chainlink fence
less a hand full of your hair
and a back with skin to claw freely
betrays you

better know how to stay in your stumbling stance
after the ear-nose-kidney combination lands perfectly

better know how to hear *I love you*
at the wrong time or from the wrong person
and smile in fluent *No.*
Better know how to hold on to what you cannot give away.

The first one to flinch
        introduces themselves as failure
The first one to flinch
        is not my mother's child
The first one to flinch
        buys the whole bar a drink
The first one to flinch
Wins.
Because it took enough of you to play
It's just   so easy though.

Who would want to win like that?

Lean In

The Moon ignores its station, floats toward my window.
Leans in…

So this is when the clouds bleed
a softer saline toward the open eyes
of the retention pool by the high school stadium.

The Lost of us look hard, the
third star on the right learned to
undertongue a razor like Bishop.

Every so often the sky, looks away
shy enough, until it asks,
what the hell you looking at?
until it pulls out a cell phone and starts filming us
like we're the police.

But that Moon tho,
thinks her face is maple syrup: the
sticky type of light teenagers fall in love to.
No one has the moxie to tell her she's wrong.
She might not be wrong.

She ain't wrong.

The Clouds only court the sad girls.
The Stars want the forever boys
to make liquor of their blood.
Not even the Sun
which knows how to warm bliss into skin-
only in the summer months, only
in the daytime, only then would he
dare challenge the Moon.

But the Sun ain't said a word.
The Flowers opened up, but got hushed,
because surely we need their color when the world takes away
so much light!

Golden Hunter, all full, makes it prettier
than a homecoming queen, but
  but yeah, She don't float,
unless the sky is willing to fall
and don't stick around for dinner.
Not even if we ask nice.

But Flower. But Moon.
But Sun. But Moon.
But Star, but Cloud, but Sky.

But that Moon tho.

Because of her, the Snow is speaking.
She eclipses it;
there's a more pressing matter
aligning.

And the Moon is gentle in the chastising,
Hush darlings, the adults are speaking now.

The Sun,
ever sexy,
shaves the Planet's long, long legs.
And the Moon
while doing a fan dance in December's mouth,
leans in…
Everyone knows you been crying, poet.
Everyone's guessed, somehow.
She might not be wrong.

She ain't wrong.

When to Un

On finding out the father of my Daughter is a Trump Supporter and closet racist

I   un-fuck   you!

You can do it.

I checked.
When the other party is a complete & utter asshole
who wants to re-elect a man that has submerged the entire American
population into a sinkhole of shit and calamity, then yep.
retroactively,   magically   with three words:
I un-fuck you!

I un-fuck you.
I un-screw you
I un-do you
I undo myself from you
I un-couple every hook and eye
          that hinged us into fling open
          and slam shut
I un-fuck you

I un-dote on you.

I un-excuse you
          for the friends who knew you only through me
& the "please forgive him for not showing up"
I un-show up for you.
I un2am you.

I un-shame, for you
I unshed the lagoon of tears   I cried
        I masked
        sank into and salt-floated above ...*for you. For you?*
For you: I un-for you!

I un-worry for you.
I un-count nights
        I lay awake wondering where you were- -
No: I un-count nights I lay awake
        knowing exactly where your trifling ass was.

I un-pray for you.

I un-appeal all the pleas
for your strength knowing you never
had to be anything but coward.

What your parents must have thought of you
by all the shit they taught you
about duck and cover,
stick and move,
slippery and slipping
fast missing your daughter's entire childhood
because you couldn't bring this Black woman home.

I un-deconstruct for you, because look at you:
How you spent us both into emotional bankruptcy.
How you built this wall around you.
How that sounds so familiar.
How you chose your idol easily.

I un-choose you.
I un-hope hopes for your growth,
I un-plan plans for your future,
I un-dream dreams for your family.

I un-concern myself with all
the fears for your safety
knowing now you
have no concern for your daughter's   or mine.

I un-ravel the best strands of me
        I knit to the mediocre of you…
and I taught your daughter too,
**that when a fuckboy be on some fuck-shit she can un-fuck them
too**
I un-fuck you as cordially as I know how
and I invite you, sir
                        …to go fuck yourself.

The Past, the Present and the Future Slam Dance

Memory is time being desperate
Now is a bloated promise
The Future is an echo laugh

Memory is time being desperate
A disco perm armed with whiskey, and midnight tears
Memory calls you baby when you need someone to velvet the rougher parts
Memory was never sober
Memory just wants you back and if you go, you die there

Memory is time being desperate
Now is a bloated promise
A hawk-eyed stare unshaken by an unmade bed and all of your neglected
chores
Now puts its feet up on the furniture
Now lights matches on the sole of its boots
Now is gonna disappear as soon as you ask for a dance.   Don't ask-
dance.

Memory is time being desperate
Now is a bloated promise
The Future is an echo laugh
No, the Christmas morning giggle of a happy child with a brand new toy
The Future is a dance too, and it makes you wonder how it moves
The Future is proud to hold your hand in public is turning into Now as
we speak.
        And soon Memory.

Are you afraid yet?

in the Time of Corona, Alone

There's a breath I save for exhaling a pain my brain
is determined to relive and if possible, make worse
in each reliving.
There's an energy I save for pep talks
I have to give myself on the days it is
difficult to motivate my limbs
toward production.
There's a pure and uncut
loneliness I save for staring at the full moon.

There's gravity I save for when I can spend it. All day in bed.

There is love, yes. People love me. Tell me so anytime
I need to hear it. I need to hear it more. There aren't
enough full moons and too many pep talks since April.
Since April began, I've watched my savings drain,
bottom out. A friend asks do I need anything, I don't say
I'm in the red. I tell a lie called fine. I breathe, move,
busy my hands

wait for the full moon.

On Becoming an Eclipse

In Which I, A Poet of a Certain Skill Level, Interrogates Imposter Syndrome

And maybe you can appreciate their existence
without them appreciating your own. But they are
doing what you want to, better than you are doing it
and resentment makes admiration
a viscous pile of waste. Looking out the window
is the worst sort of mirror.

This isn't about loving something
but possessing it; the fear that you will have nothing
makes you hold on to the wrong thing.

Once, you swallowed the moon whole.
Another time, you nibbled it down bite by bite.
And another time still, you
leaned out your tongue,
flipped the full moon
into your ready mouth,
genuflected and refused the sacrificial wine.

You could not taste the difference.

You became a myth   or an eclipse; the caution that good parents give
to their babies:
*Someone said **fraud**, and she answered to it, shamefully*
watched the sky suffer too many long nights without shine. Who does that?

And then you realize that every single time you've said
you, you meant **I.**
You've been doing that to your **I** the whole time.
I have had time to learn to taste the difference
or

No one can tell my story better than I can:

So, I parted my lips
and the lilt of pale fell, a shy beam but
stronger with each octave I sung.
And braver still: I crooned myself a shave of incandescence
anyone could fall in love to; Pianoforte
now and long until I pulled the moon from my belly
I became
the once dark eclipse choosing
to move out of the shadows, or out of my own way into
my very own sky.

Advice from the Better Angels

this room loves you all skin gown,
hip hug,
proper drape   comfort   wish for that

air in this room is want with worship
doesn't let you breathe above your pay grade
serves this now kind of you   wish for that

you're in the room now, all the time
with 7000 thoughts and an exhale
you won't let go… let go   wish for that

when this room was built, it was in his rule
when this room was love it was a black garland wrapping your hair into
whisper
when you were here, in this room, wishing for what you have now
you did more with your mind than you do with your ass
like anybody goes to a pity party on purpose
even one with clever decorations

it isn't easy to lift a fog with your two bare hands
it takes extraordinary power
where's your power?   wish for that

what waits outside the door is a bitter crush
        and a darlinged memory
what waits in here swallows your deepest purple
        and hands you a lung full of doubt
what you haven't learned becomes a tenderness
what you would not fear, scream it out
what does this room wish for you?
you know the answer. wish for that.

Medicine

(after the last scene of Medicine for the Melancholy)

This is what it's like when the color
returns: broken promises, bad
lighting. The couchbed sucking
your face, cheek first into a yellow
hickey. And she always runs,
a teared-up eye shedding its burn.
She will always run.

Once the body unlearns shock,
fluently,
trust becomes a
theme park
fairytale.
The rubble of it.
The tumble dust.
Lilting voice in a bicycle spoke-
she will always run. Look at it.

Don't ever look away.

An Aubade for Midnights Too

As if the morning isn't also dark too
A midnight reaching up and out, and then through
As if the morning isn't also dark too
When December embraces the crystal cracking dew
As if the fecundity of gray rain clouds
does not painfully labor through lightning and loud
a necessary nebulous to confuse night to concede.
If sunrise be the goal, then midnight meets a need.
As if endurance scares us all but enduring makes us proud.
A million wished-on stars, come sky to crowd
As if morning isn't also dark too
A bliss to bless, a reckon to review

And Maybe, Community

I whisper your name at the stretch of sky that lingers above you
I do not believe in a thick gray chunk of earned elements
assigned to steal the joy
from our place on the planet
But I do know from every cloud puff there is promise: cyclical, renewal
There is a cerulean sustenance shaded into an above we all share breath in
A shock of blue shot through with what makes me myself and is uniquely you
I may not believe in much
but I believe
in that

I say with my most honest self
Give us a good ground to trod, to trudge
Give us great sky to aspire to touch
Give us community like a song
        we are surprised we already know the lyrics to
Give us relationship.
It is difficult to destroy anything you've named for yourself.

When they tell me to say their names, I whisper yours too
I do not believe the heart breaks without creating more space
for love and for hope to populate.
Properly honoring past informs how we treat our tomorrow
I do know there is a something around us that makes us just as well as it
can undo us;
it is asking us to choose!
There is a promise of collaboration in the connection we all coexist in.
I may not believe in much
but I believe
in us
I believe in this.
I believe in all of you

About the Author

Angelique Palmer is a performance poet, a finalist in the 2015 Women of the World Poetry Slam, and a member of the 2017 Busboys and Poets/ Beltway Poetry Slam Team. Author of *The Chambermaid's Style Guide*, and *Also Dark* (Etruscan Press), she is a Florida State University Creative Writing graduate who calls northern Virginia home. Her work centers on Black Femme Narratives, Awkward Queerness, and Mental Health and Recovery. She makes her own ice cream.

Books from Etruscan Press

Zarathustra Must Die | Dorian Alexander
The Disappearance of Seth | Kazim Ali
The Last Orgasm | Nin Andrews
Drift Ice | Jennifer Atkinson
Crow Man | Tom Bailey
Coronology | Claire Bateman
Topographies | Stephen Benz
What We Ask of Flesh | Remica L. Bingham
The Greatest Jewish-American Lover in Hungarian History | Michael Blumenthal
No Hurry | Michael Blumenthal
Choir of the Wells | Bruce Bond
Cinder | Bruce Bond
The Other Sky | Bruce Bond and Aron Wiesenfeld
Peal | Bruce Bond
Scar | Bruce Bond
Poems and Their Making: A Conversation | Moderated by Philip Brady
Crave: Sojourn of a Hungry Soul | Laurie Jean Cannady
Toucans in the Arctic | Scott Coffel
Sixteen | Auguste Corteau
Wattle & daub | Brian Coughlan
Body of a Dancer | Renée E. D'Aoust
Ill Angels | Dante Di Stefano
Aard-vark to Axolotl: Pictures From my Grandfather's Dictionary | Karen Donovan
Trio: Planet Parable, Run: A Verse-History of Victoria Woodhull, and Endless Body | Karen Donovan, Diane Raptosh, and Daneen Wardrop
Scything Grace | Sean Thomas Dougherty
Areas of Fog | Will Dowd
Romer | Robert Eastwood
Wait for God to Notice | Sari Fordham
Surrendering Oz | Bonnie Friedman
Nahoonkara | Peter Grandbois
Triptych: The Three-Legged World, In Time, and Orpheus & Echo | Peter Grandbois, James McCorkle, and Robert Miltner
The Candle: Poems of Our 20th Century Holocausts | William Heyen
The Confessions of Doc Williams & Other Poems | William Heyen
The Football Corporations | William Heyen
A Poetics of Hiroshima | William Heyen
September 11, 2001: American Writers Respond | Edited by William Heyen
Shoah Train | William Heyen
American Anger: An Evidentiary | H. L. Hix
As Easy As Lying | H. L. Hix

Etruscan Press Is Proud of Support Received From

Wilkes University

Youngstown State University

Ohio Arts Council

The Stephen & Jeryl Oristaglio Foundation

Community of Literary Magazines and Presses

[clmp]

National Endowment for the Arts

Drs. Barbara Brothers & Gratia Murphy Endowment

The Thendara Foundation

Founded in 2001 with a generous grant from the Oristaglio Foundation, Etruscan Press is a nonprofit cooperative of poets and writers working to produce and promote books that nurture the dialogue among genres, achieve a distinctive voice, and reshape the literary and cultural histories of which we are a part.

etruscan press
www.etruscanpress.org

Etruscan Press books may be ordered from

Consortium Book Sales and Distribution
800.283.3572
www.cbsd.com

Etruscan Press is a 501(c)(3) nonprofit organization.
Contributions to Etruscan Press are tax deductible
as allowed under applicable law.
For more information, a prospectus,
or to order one of our titles,
contact us at books@etruscanpress.org.